VOTES FOR WOMEN

Diane Atkinson

Education Department at the Museum of London

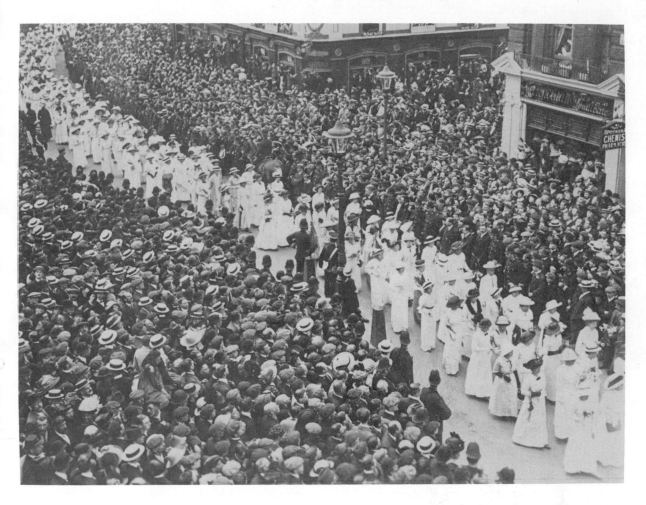

CAMBRIDGE UNIVERSITY PRESS
Cambridge
New York   Port Chester   Melbourne   Sydney

To my mother and father

Published by the Press Syndicate of the University of Cambridge
The Pitt Building, Trumpington Street, Cambridge CB2 1RP
40 West 20th Street, New York, NY 10011, USA
10 Stamford Road, Oakleigh, Melbourne 3166, Australia

© Cambridge University Press 1988

First published 1988
Third printing 1990

Printed in Great Britain at the University Press, Cambridge

British Library cataloguing in publication data
Atkinson, Diane
  Votes for women – (Women in history).
  1. Women – Suffrage – Great Britain – History
  I. Title II. Series
  324.6′23′0941 JN979

Library of Congress cataloguing in publication data
Atkinson, Diane.
  Votes for women/Diane Atkinson.
  1. Women – Suffrage – Great Britain – History.
  I. Title.
  JN979.A86 1988
     87-33637
  324.6′23′0941—dc19   CIP

ISBN 0 521 31044 X

VN

Acknowledgements

The author and publisher would like to thank
the following for permission to reproduce
illustrations:
The Fawcett Library/City of London
Polytechnic pp.11 (*top right and bottom left*), 23
(*top*), 42, 43 (*top left*); *Ada Nield Chew: The Life
and Writings of a Working Woman*, presented by
Doris Nield Chew, Virago, 1982, p.11 (*top
left*); Horace Carter, Documentary
Photographic Archive, Manchester Polytechnic
p.13
We should especially like to thank The
Museum of London for their help in providing
the other photographs for this book.

Note
The words which appear in italic in the text
are explained in the glossary on page 48.

Cover illustration campaigning for Votes for
Women: Mrs Rose Lamartine Yates and her
son (The Museum of London).
Title page procession of suffragettes at Emily
Wilding Davison's funeral, 1913 (The Museum
of London).

Contents

"The Suffragette," March 13, 1914.

Registered at the G.P.O. as a Newspaper.

The
Suffragette

Edited by Christabel Pankhurst.

The Official Organ of the
Women's Social and Political Union.

No. 74—Vol. II.   FRIDAY, MARCH 13, 1914.   Price 1d. Weekly (Post Free) ·1½d.

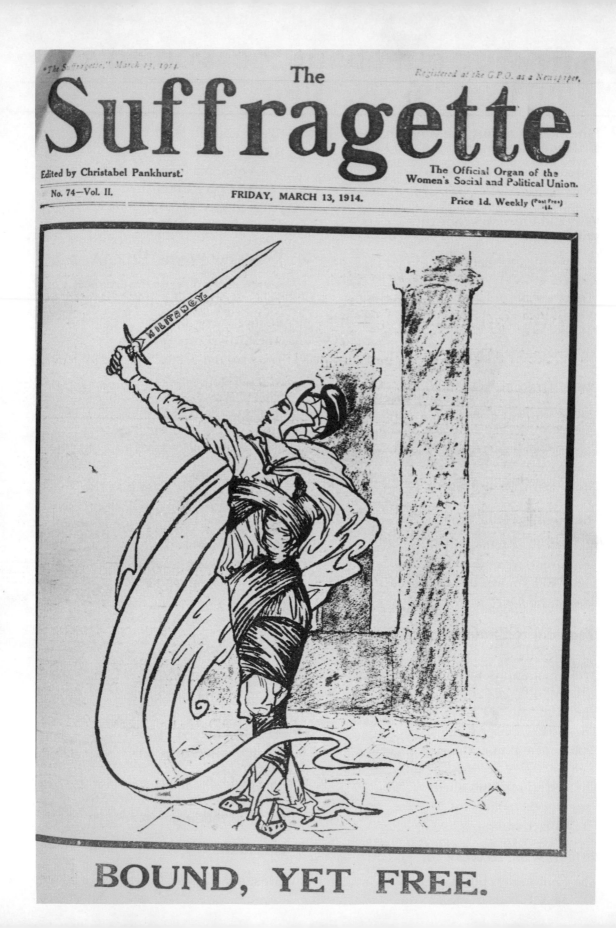

BOUND, YET FREE.

1 Finding out about the women's suffrage movement

Introduction

A lot of people think that the fight for votes for women began and ended with the Pankhurst family. Most have heard about Emily Wilding Davison, the woman who threw herself at the King's horse at the Derby in 1913, or know about the women who smashed windows and burned down houses and churches. Of course there is a great deal more to the story. This book attempts to tell the story of two very different campaigns to win the vote. The more moderate and peaceful struggle was waged by *suffragists*, members of the *National Union of Women's Suffrage Societies (NUWSS)*. Those women who used militant tactics and were members of the *Women's Social and Political Union (WSPU)* were called *suffragettes*.

Votes for women was a major breakthrough which affected the lives of *all* women in Britain. Once women were given the vote, they were able for the first time to exert strong pressure on their local MPs to fight for women's interests in Parliament.

Evidence

Here are the different kinds of sources which have been used in writing this book.

Newspapers

The two main women's suffrage societies had three newspapers of their own: *The Common Cause* (NUWSS), *Votes for Women* (WSPU) and *The Suffragette* (WSPU). These weekly papers show how the two very different campaigns were run. National and local newspapers also reported the activities of the suffrage campaigners, their processions, demonstrations and fund-raising events.

Bound, Yet Free. *By 1914 many a suffragette saw herself as a modern-day Joan of Arc. St Joan was the patron saint of the WSPU.*

Diaries and personal correspondence

Most of the personalities involved in the struggle for the vote kept diaries and wrote letters to friends and colleagues. They give a good insight into the day-to-day aspects of the campaign, and they sometimes reflect a person's more private feelings.

Autobiographies and biographies

Most of the senior members of the movement wrote their own accounts, or had biographies written about them during or after the campaigning.

Written and visual propaganda

All the societies produced a lot of propaganda which was intended to convert public opinion to their side. The WSPU and NUWSS attracted several talented women artists who gave their skills free of charge to the cause, and produced clever, visual propaganda in the form of banners, posters and postcards.

Photographs

Hundreds of photographs of major events and people in the movement were taken during the campaign. They appeared in the suffragettes' newspapers, national and local papers, and were sold to supporters of the cause.

Hansard

Hansard is a detailed written account of what MPs say in the House of Commons. We can find out a lot about the views of individual politicians, and how they changed, if at all, as each successive women's suffrage *bill* was debated.

Home Office papers

Government papers show how the *Cabinet*, the *Metropolitan Police* and the *Home Office* looked upon suffrage demonstrations, how they should be policed and how the offenders should be dealt with in prison.

2 Why did women want the vote?

The position of women in the 19th century

- Until 1839 a woman who was divorced from her husband was not allowed to see her children unless she had an 'unblemished' character. The *Custody of Infants Act*, 1839, gave more rights to divorced women to see their children. But the father still had almost complete control of the children.

- 1842 *Factory Act:* women in textile factories were to work no more than 12 hours a day.

- 1847 *Factory Act:* women in textile factories were to work no more than 10 hours a day.

- Until 1857 divorce was not possible as we know it today. A divorce could only be obtained by an act of Parliament or through the Church courts, for very special reasons. The *Divorce Act*, 1857, gave husbands the right to divorce their wives on the grounds of adultery, but women could not divorce for the same reasons until 1923.

- Until 1870 a married woman was not allowed to keep any of her earnings. Her husband owned all her money, belongings and clothes. The *Married Women's Property Act*, 1870, allowed women to keep £200 of their own earnings.

- In 1871 Newnham College, Cambridge, was founded and the first women were admitted to Cambridge University (although they were not allowed the same degrees as men until 1949).

- In 1873 all women were allowed to see their children if they got divorced from their husbands.

- Until 1884 a married woman was considered a 'chattel' (possession) of her husband.

- In 1888 the first strike of unskilled women workers took place in Britain. Anne Besant, a well-known socialist, led the 'Match Girls' out on strike at Bryant and May's match factory in London. They demanded better pay and conditions. The publicity forced the company to improve the Match Girls' conditions of work.

During the 19th century, women struggled to improve their legal position in society. By 1900, as this list indicates, there had been a slow but steady improvement in the legal position of women. Important laws were passed which began to redress some, though not all, of the legal inequalities which they faced in everyday life.

Women at work

Women from all social classes, not just the poorest, were demanding widespread reforms. The problem of low pay (women generally earned half, or less than half, of a man's wage

The exploitation of women as cheap labour was a recurring theme in WSPU propaganda.

A comparison of men's and women's wages

Occupation	Men's wages (average)	Women's wages (average)
Thimble-makers – brass, 1851	15–21s a week	7–9s a week
Surface workers at tin mines, 1880s	2s a day	1s a day
Machinists in tailoring, 1880s	22s 6d a week	11s a week
Office work, 1880s	£2+ a week	£1 a week
Domestic service, 1880s	£35 a year (valet, man's personal servant)	£10–16 a year (house maid)
Printing, 1880s	7½–8d an hour	5–6d an hour
Carpet weavers, 1890s	35s a week	20s a week
Civil Service typists, 1914	£3 a week	£1 a week

Wages are in shillings (s) and old pence (d)
12d = 1s (5 new pence)
20s = £1 (100 new pence)

Figures based on a variety of sources: Mine Account Books; Board of Trade Enquiry into the Earnings and Hours of the Workpeople of the United Kingdom, 1909; The Royal Commission on Labour 1893–4; Mrs Beeton's Book of Household Management; Morning Chronicle surveys.

for doing exactly the same job) cut across all areas of employment, from teaching, office work and nursing, to domestic service and factory work. As well as struggling for better pay, women were fighting for the right to become doctors and lawyers, apprentices in certain trades, and have proper technical training.

The new popular newspapers of the 1890s reported the horrific poverty of many working-class families. Many of the poorest and most exploited people were women. By 1900 there were over five million wage-earning women in Britain, most of them grossly underpaid. The worst cases of women being used as cheap labour were of those who worked at home, especially in the East End of London. For example, at the turn of the century matchbox makers would have had to complete 15,000 matchboxes to earn 20s. Most of them in fact earned 12s (60 new pence) a week.

These issues of poverty and inequality formed the background of the demand for votes for women.

The growth in parliamentary democracy

By the turn of the century, 7 million men, that is two-thirds of all adult men in England and Wales, could vote. Many of them were working-class. Party politicians were very much aware of this fact when representing their policies. While all trade unions

Who got the vote?

1832   *The Great Reform Act* gave the vote to half a million more men. Middle-class men could now vote as well as landowners. In total about one-fifth of all men were given the vote. But the Act now specifically excluded women. By using the term 'male person' for the first time in English history, women were legally prevented from voting in parliamentary elections.

1867   *The Second Reform Act* gave the vote to about 2.5 million male householders out of a total population of 22 million. John Stuart Mill, MP for Westminster, made the first plea for women's suffrage in Parliament. Dr Richard Pankhurst gave many examples of women voting for MPs in the past, certainly in medieval times. No progress made on votes for women.

1884   *The Third Reform Act* entitled about 5 million men in all (nearly two-thirds of the male population) to vote. Large numbers of working men were given the chance to vote for their MP, who could, in theory, represent their interests in Parliament. (Those who could not vote were: the poorest men, servants who lived in the homes of their employers, criminals and patients in lunatic asylums.) Again, no progress on votes for women.

appreciated the need for votes for everyone, they felt at that time that their priority was *not* to actively support women's suffrage, but to work for votes for all men first and foremost. Put alongside the size of the existing electorate the women's claim was certainly conservative in its scope. They were prepared to accept, in the first stage at least, votes for around one million women. Other women would get the vote later, once the sex barrier had been removed.

Why did women want the vote?

Women fought for the vote as a means to an end. The vote had been a key factor in safeguarding the interests of men, and now women were demanding the same. Little progress could be made to improve women's working conditions, for example, until MPs were made accountable to female voters. Mrs Emmeline Pankhurst, a leading suffragette, said of the vote, 'first of all it is a symbol, secondly a safeguard, and thirdly an instrument'.

There were of course many people, men and women, who strongly disagreed with the idea of votes for women. They came from all social classes, and held very different political views.

Thousands of handbills like this one of 1907 were given away by the NUWSS and WSPU

Why Women Want the Vote.

BECAUSE

No race or class or sex can have its interest properly safeguarded in the legislature of a country unless it is represented by direct suffrage.

BECAUSE

Politics and economics go hand in hand. And so long as woman has no political status she will be the "bottom dog" as a wage-earner.

BECAUSE

While men who are voters can get their economic grievances listened to, non-voters are disregarded.

BECAUSE

The possession of citizenship and the meeting together for political discussion stimulates the faculty for combined action, and gives of itself a greater power of economic resistance.

BECAUSE

Women are taxed without being represented, and taxation without representation is tyranny.

BECAUSE

Women have to obey the laws equally with men, and they ought to have a voice in deciding what those laws shall be.

BECAUSE

The Legislature in the past has not made laws which are equal between men and women; and these laws will not be altered till women get the vote.

BECAUSE

All the more important and lucrative positions are barred to them, and opportunities of public service are denied.

BECAUSE

Politics have invaded the home, and woman must therefore enter politics.

BECAUSE

Grave questions, such as the death rate of infants, the waste of child-life, the employment of married women, unemployment, wages and care of the aged, cannot be satisfactorily settled if the women's point of view is left out.

BECAUSE

All the wisest men and women realise that decisions based upon the point of view of men and women together are more valuable than those based upon either singly.

BECAUSE

So long as the majority of the women of the country have no interest in politics, the children grow up ignorant of the meaning of the struggle for freedom, and lessons learnt in one generation by bitter experience have to be relearnt by the next in the same school.

BECAUSE

Wherever women have become voters, reform has proceeded more rapidly than before, and even at home our municipal government, in which the women have a certain share, is in advance and not behind our Parliamentary attitude on many important questions.

BECAUSE

Women, like men, need to have some interests outside the home, and will be better comrades to their husbands, better mothers to their children, and better housekeepers of the home, when they get them.

From the " Reformers' Year Book," 1907.

It is probably true to say that by the turn of the century the actual number of people who wanted women's suffrage was a tiny minority of the population as a whole. The vast majority were still against it.

Opposition to women's suffrage

The main reason why women had not won the vote by the early 20th century, after nearly 40 years of campaigning, was because most politicians were not committed to the idea. Most wanted women to have the vote only if their party benefited from it. Conservative MPs generally believed in keeping things the way they had always been. They also feared that women, given the chance, might vote for the Liberals, or for the new Labour Party.

The Liberals in general believed that women should have the vote, but they too were afraid that new women voters would support the main opposition party, the Conservatives, or the Labour Party. The idea of property-owning women getting the vote sent shivers down the backs of most Liberal politicians. Although Herbert Henry Asquith, Liberal Prime Minister from 1908 until 1916, was a committed *Anti*, there was a large percentage of Liberals who supported and worked hard for votes for women.

The Labour Party was a new party begun in 1892 to represent working men in Parliament. It was afraid that unless *all* adults got the vote, the party would not benefit from any changes in the *franchise*. If property-owning women got the vote, but not working-class women, the Conservatives and Liberals would gain an important advantage. While the Labour Party was committed to the idea of adult suffrage (that is votes for all men and women), many felt that all men should have the vote first.

There were of course many people who opposed the idea of women's *suffrage*. They were known as the 'Antis'. Here are some of the reasons they gave:

- women would be corrupted by politics, and chivalry would die out
- if women became involved in politics, they would stop marrying, having

children, and the human race would die out
- women were emotional creatures, and incapable of making a sound political decision

These reasons may seem ludicrous to us, but at the time were taken seriously by a wide cross-section of women as well as men. But in each political party there were supporters of votes for women. Unfortunately the numbers were small, and all too often the promises of support which were made to the women's suffrage campaigners turned out to be token gestures.

The international scene

There was a very strong international aspect to the women's suffrage movement. In countries with a well-established system of parliamentary democracy, women were struggling for the right to vote. The WSPU and the NUWSS had particularly close links with countries that had already given women the right to vote, and where there were vigorous suffrage campaigns underway. Several States in the USA, most of Australia, New Zealand, and even the Isle of Man had enfranchised women in the 19th century. (see page 45). Activists from these countries came to Britain and worked within the NUWSS and the WSPU and advised them on the tactics they should use.

The visitors gave speeches on how the vote had improved the living and working conditions and wages of women, and men too, in their own countries. It was pointed out that votes for women benefited *everyone*, not just women. If women's wages increased as a result of the vote, for example, men's wages would increase too.

The International Women's Suffrage Alliance was founded in 1902, and organised conferences in places such as Washington (1902), Berlin (1904) and Copenhagen (1906). Susan B. Anthony, a well-known American *feminist* and suffragist, was the President of the organisation, and the English suffragist Mrs Fawcett was a member of the senior executive. All over the world women's fight for the vote seemed to be getting stronger.

9

3 The suffragists

Who were the suffragists?

The suffragists were a group of people who campaigned to win the vote for women. They were mainly women, but men were also involved in the campaign. The suffragists used peaceful, moderate and law-abiding methods. By the end of the 19th century their main organisation was called the National Union of Women's Suffrage Societies (NUWSS). Their aims were simple and straightforward: 'To promote the claim of women to the Parliamentary vote on the same terms as it is or may be granted to men.' They did not demand the vote for *all* women, but they wanted women to be placed on an equal footing with the men who already had it, and the men who would be given it in the future. They did not want to be linked to any one political party.

The growth of the suffrage movement

Although the issue of votes for women had first been raised in the 1830s it was not until the 1860s that a tiny women's suffrage movement was founded in five of the major cities in Britain: London, Manchester, Bristol, Birmingham and Edinburgh. After nearly 40 years of peaceful campaigning, collecting petitions, lobbying for support from MPs, and holding numerous drawing-room meetings, the vote for women was no nearer. Most politicians did not take the demand at all seriously, and all too often it was treated with ridicule when discussed in the House of Commons.

Although membership of the women's suffrage societies was for women only, some men did join in the demand for justice and equal citizenship for women. John Stuart Mill, MP for Westminster, first raised the issue in Parliament when he demanded that women be given the vote in the 1867 Reform Act, an Act which created over half a million new male voters. His proposal was defeated and for 30 years little more was heard of the demand for women's suffrage. However, John Stuart Mill and other male supporters provided an important example for other men to follow. By 1901 men were playing a small, though important, role in the campaign.

The suffragists worked hard to win support for the idea of votes for women in London and the major cities and towns. From the beginning the north of England was in the forefront of the fight for the vote. In 1867 Lydia Becker helped to form the Manchester Society for Women's Suffrage, and for many years she wrote and lectured on the 'struggle', organised several petitions which were presented to MPs at the House of Commons, and for 20 years edited the *Women's Suffrage Journal*.

The NUWSS was formed in 1897. Mrs Millicent Garrett Fawcett was its President. The NUWSS carried on in much the same style as the societies founded 30 years earlier. Propaganda work was carried out quietly and peacefully, women were trained as speakers for the cause, and local women were paid to organise the movement in their area. Members of the NUWSS decided the policies, and elected the President and a national *executive committee*. By 1914 there were over 600 member societies, more than 100,000 individual members, and the NUWSS was the oldest and largest national organisation campaigning for votes for women.

Factory workers and the 'radical suffragists'

In the 1890s a group of women within the NUWSS worked hard to get the vote for working-class women. To these women, who became known as the *radical suffragists*, the vote had to be more than a symbol of equality; the lives of working-class women *had* to improve.

The movement for working-class women's suffrage was founded and did particularly well

Ada Nield Chew: a working-class suffragist from Staffordshire. She joined the NUWSS in 1908 and became a full-time, paid organiser in Lancashire.

Eva Gore-Booth (left) and her sister Constance. Eva was a key figure in the radical suffrage movement in the North of England, based in Manchester. She helped to recruit thousands of factory women, mainly cotton mill workers, into the suffrage movement. The two sisters were well-educated Irish women from a wealthy and aristocratic background.

Millicent Garrett Fawcett: President of the NUWSS for over 20 years. Her sister, Elizabeth Garrett Anderson, was the first woman to qualify as a doctor in Britain.

in north-west England, in the cotton towns of Lancashire and Cheshire (see map on p. 14). The radical suffragists encouraged hundreds of female cotton workers to join the NUWSS. Dinner-hour meetings were held at the mill gates and outside factories. Towns like Bolton, Blackburn, Rochdale and Preston were key centres for the spinning and weaving of cotton. Here support for the radical suffragists was at its strongest. One of the NUWSS branches describes their work:

Workers have been sent about the factory districts to hold open-air meetings and to speak to the women at the factory gates and in their own houses. This work is necessarily slow as the area to be covered is very large but all our workers report themselves convinced that the women feel a real interest in the subject, many of them, particularly those who are rate-payers, keenly resent their exclusion from the franchise . . . There is no difficulty in obtaining signatures, only a very small proportion refuse to sign. But there is a

11

great deal of hard work involved going from house to house in the evening after factory hours, holding cottage meetings and collecting signatures.

North of England Society for Women's Suffrage **Annual Report**, *1899/1900*

These women joined a movement which up till then was dominated by genteel, well-educated, middle-class women who felt frustrated at their restricted lives. Many factory workers, especially those in the cotton mills, wanted the vote to raise their low wages and improve their dreadful living and working conditions.

By 1900 female cotton workers were the highest paid factory women in Britain. In most cotton mills they easily outnumbered male workers, often by two to one. Many of them were involved in trade union activities but they had little power within the trades union movement which was particularly hostile to married women who worked.

By 1900 the radical suffragists were in a good position. Many of their followers had gained valuable experience as canvassers over the years. Some were members of the *Women's Co-operative Guild*, and others were public speakers who toured the country on bicycles, or in horse-drawn caravans. Their experience helped them a great deal in the women's suffrage campaign and this made a big impact on the NUWSS and other groups.

The interest in women's suffrage grew quickly in the north of England:

In the cotton districts during the summer months the workers spend their evenings out of doors, more after the fashion of the Continent than English towns, and on certain nights in the week anyone going into the market place can get an audience of interested and intelligent men and women varying from six hundred to a thousand and even fifteen hundred who will stand for an hour or two to hear the question discussed.

The National Union of Women's Suffrage Societies **Annual Report**, *1903*

The suffragists canvassed from door to door, and spoke at local trades union meetings. More suffrage committees were set up to co-ordinate the campaign locally and nationally. Working-class women continued to join the radical suffrage movement in large numbers.

Some of the committees were made up exclusively of female cotton workers, and a number became paid organisers and speakers.

In 1903 the very first organisation to be set up specifically to campaign for votes for working-class women was founded by Esther Roper and Eva Gore-Booth. It was called the Lancashire and Cheshire Women Textile and Other Workers Representation Committee. They tried to get support from Liberal politicians, the trades union movement, and the Labour Party (still a small party at this time). The Pankhurst family were actively involved with this organisation, and Christabel, who later became co-founder and leader of the WSPU, learned a lot from Esther Roper and Eva Gore-Booth.

Of all the women's suffrage societies, the peaceful NUWSS movement had the most to offer working-class women. It was quite common for working-class mothers involved in the campaign to take their children with them while they went out canvassing for support, or when attending and speaking at public meetings. Travelling speakers put up with a great deal of discomfort, often sleeping on floors, and many endured abuse from people who disagreed with their views. However, for many women the feelings of excitement and pride in their struggle for the vote kept them going during the long hours of work, the inevitable disappointments and occasional hostility from their families and close friends.

Other suffragist societies

Alongside the work of the NUWSS, a number of other societies worked hard for the women's suffrage movement. After 1907 over 20 new women's suffrage societies were formed, representing a wide cross-section of professional, religious and political opinions. Their headquarters were usually in London, and some of them had branches in other major towns and cities. Working-class and professional women (1905), gymnastic teachers (1908), civil servants (1911) and women teachers (1912), all had their own societies. Other professional women such as the Artists' Suffrage League (1907), the Actresses' Franchise League (1908), and the Women

Writers' Suffrage League (1908) publicised votes for women. Their talents were used to the full. Banners, postcards and posters were produced by women artists. Members of the Actresses' Franchise League wrote and appeared in plays such as *How the Vote was Won*, and *Lady Geraldine's Speech*, which were performed in private drawing-rooms, and various theatres around Britain.

Groups of Catholics, Quakers, Anglicans and Jews ran their own societies for women's suffrage. Scottish, Welsh and Irish suffragists had their own organisations and sent their members on all the large demonstrations. Liberal, Conservative and Socialist supporters of votes for women added their voices to the fight, and the Men's League for Women's Suffrage (1907), and the Men's Political Union for Women's Enfranchisement (1910) gave support to both sides of the women's suffrage movement.

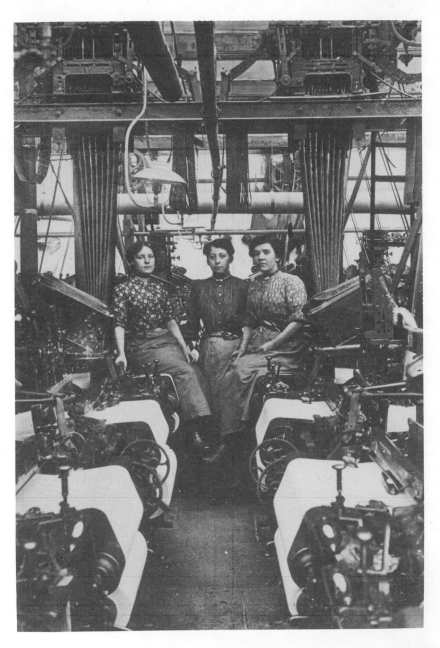

Lancashire Lassies having a Minute. *Thousands of women, like the three cotton workers who are posing here, joined the women's suffrage movement.*

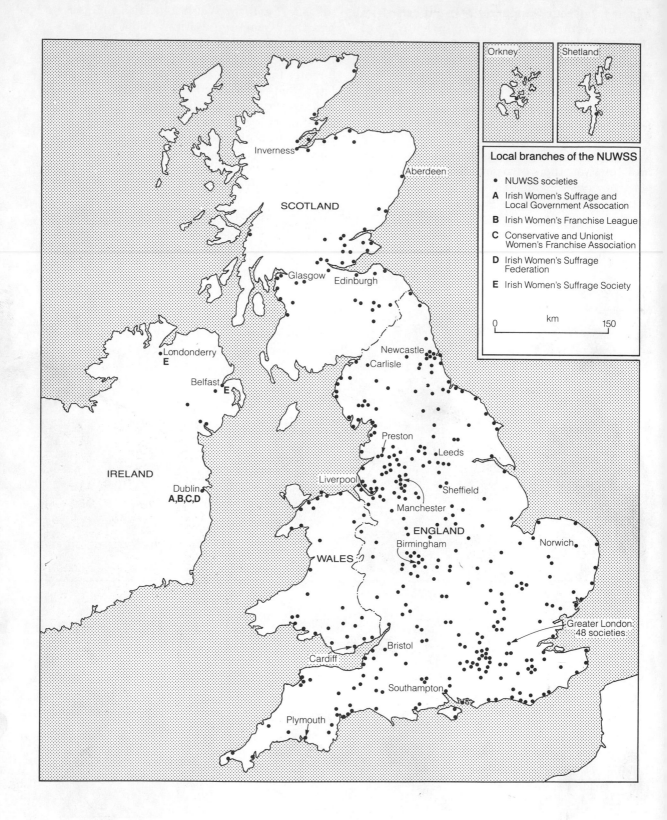

Orkney

Shetland

Local branches of the NUWSS

- • NUWSS societies
- **A** Irish Women's Suffrage and Local Government Assocation
- **B** Irish Women's Franchise League
- **C** Conservative and Unionist Women's Franchise Association
- **D** Irish Women's Suffrage Federation
- **E** Irish Women's Suffrage Society

0   km   150

Inverness

Aberdeen

SCOTLAND

Glasgow

Edinburgh

Newcastle

Carlisle

Londonderry
E

Belfast
E

Preston

Leeds

Liverpool

Sheffield

IRELAND

Manchester

Dublin
A,B,C,D

ENGLAND

Birmingham

Norwich

WALES

Greater London: 48 societies

Bristol

Cardiff

Southampton

Plymouth

4 The suffragettes

Who were the suffragettes?

The suffragettes were members of the Women's Social and Political Union (WSPU), a new women's suffrage organisation. Founded in Manchester in 1903 by the Pankhurst family, the approach was very different from the moderate and law-abiding NUWSS. In her autobiography Mrs Pankhurst described their aims:

> . . . to secure for women the Parliamentary vote as it is or may be granted to men . . . to limit our membership exclusively to women and to be satisfied with nothing but action on our question. Deeds, not Words, was to be our permanent motto.

Mrs E. Pankhurst, **My Own Story**, *1914*

Because of their actions and style of campaigning they became known as the 'suffragettes', a name given to them by the *Daily Mail* newspaper in 1906.

The early days of the WSPU

The WSPU was founded in 1903. Mrs Pankhurst explained the situation at that time:

> We clearly perceived that the new government calling themselves Liberal, were . . . hostile to women's suffrage, and would have to be fought until they were conquered or driven from office . . . I shall have to point out exactly wherein our society differs from all other suffrage associations. In the first place, our members are absolutely single-minded; they concentrate all their forces on one object, political equality with men. No member of the WSPU divides her attention between suffrage and other social reforms.

Mrs E. Pankhurst, **My Own Story**, *1914*

On 13 October 1905, at the Free Trade Hall in Manchester, the WSPU deliberately set themselves apart from all other women's suffrage societies. Christabel Pankhurst and Annie Kenney were both arrested for their

*The founders and leaders of the WSPU: Mrs Emmeline Pankhurst and her daughters Christabel (*middle*) and Sylvia (right). Mrs Pankhurst was an international celebrity. She went on hunger strike, but was too well-known a figure to be force-fed. Her daughter, Christabel, became co-leader and policy-maker of the militant WSPU movement. In 1912 she had to flee to Paris to avoid arrest for conspiring to incite violence. Sylvia's style of campaigning was very different. After a row with her mother and sister in 1914, she was thrown out of the WSPU, and continued her work for the East London Federation of Suffragettes.*

protest at a huge Liberal meeting. At the meeting they shouted, 'Will the Liberal Government give the vote to women?' This and other questions were ignored. Eventually the two protesters were thrown out of the meeting, and later were charged with offences committed in the street. Both women realised that to get the publicity their cause needed, their behaviour would have to be bad enough to get them sent to prison. Annie Kenney was sentenced to three days in prison for obstruction and disorderly behaviour, and Christabel ten days for hitting and spitting at policemen who were trying to arrest her. Shock waves were felt at such 'unwomanly' behaviour.

For three years the WSPU did valuable propaganda work in the cotton towns of the north of England. Dinner-hour meetings at factory and mill gates and door-to-door canvassing recruited working women's support for the cause. The Pankhursts were helped by Teresa Billington, a teacher from Blackburn, Annie Kenney and her sisters, all mill workers from Oldham, and Hannah Mitchell, a dressmaker's apprentice from Bolton. They worked hard to get the WSPU's message across. Hannah Mitchell wrote:

It was a wonderful experience, like putting a match to a ready built fire. The Yorkshire women rose to the call and followed us in hundreds . . . There was a unity of purpose in the suffrage movement which made social distinction seem of little importance.

Hannah Mitchell, **The Hard Way Up**, *c. 1945*

The WSPU moves to London

In many ways 1906 was a very important year for the women's suffrage movement. The Liberal party had won a landslide victory in the General Election, and the entire suffrage movement was optimistic about the prospect of votes for women in the not too distant future. Sylvia Pankhurst remembered feeling at the time, 'There was a great cry that the long reign of reaction [i.e. Conservative Party's rule] was at an end. That new ideals and new policies were to arise.'

Annie Kenney: the only working-class woman to get a senior position in the WSPU.

Emmeline Pethick Lawrence: treasurer of the WSPU. She allowed her large country house to be used as a retreat for suffragettes who were exhausted from their campaigning.

Later that year the WSPU moved its headquarters from Manchester to London, operating at first from a two-room office at 4 Clement's Inn in the Strand. It was a good spot, close to Fleet Street and the Law Courts, and not too far away from the House of Commons at Westminster. The decision to move had been an obvious one. The nation had to be 'roused' to take an interest in votes for women, and this could best be spearheaded from the capital, the home of Parliament and central government.

Rise up women!

Clement's Inn was the centre of suffragette operations. From here the plans of the WSPU were turned into direct action. Politicians were to be interrupted and questioned, Liberal MPs were to be challenged and ridiculed during *by-election* campaigns, notices of meetings had to be chalked on pavements, 'suffragette scouts' on bicycles had to go out and rouse the suburbs. Large indoor and outdoor meetings were to be organised, and propaganda had to be written and distributed all over Britain. Working-class women were to be recruited at dinner-hour meetings outside factory gates. The first London branch of the WSPU was opened in 1906 in Canning Town, a working-class district in the docks.

A lot of money was needed to finance a nation-wide campaign and hundreds of volunteers had to be recruited to do the day-to-day work, and win support for votes for women. Demonstrations, deputations to Parliament, exhibitions and bazaars were organised from the headquarters. 'Speakers classes' provided help for members who wanted to take a more public role within the movement. *Ju-jitsu* (judo) lessons were offered for those who 'wished to repel hooligan attacks'. 'At Home' meetings and the weekly newspaper *Votes for Women* kept supporters informed, and recruited new members to the organisation. Collections of money, and donations of jewellery which were sold for the cause, added to the campaign fund. Money

Many WSPU shops like this one opened in towns and cities all over Britain. They sold a wide range of items, usually in the WSPU colours of purple, white and green. Popular lines were Votes for Women chocolate, Votes for Women tea and Votes for Women marmalade.

was vital to the success of the movement.
Within eighteen months of the opening of
Clement's Inn, suffragettes could be easily
identified while on 'active service' for their
cause. Wherever and whenever possible they
were to wear the three colours of the Union:
purple, white and green. Purple stood for
dignity, white for purity, and green for hope
for the future.

The hard-working suffragettes kept the
militant movement going:

Nuns in a convent were not watched over and
supervised more strictly than were the organisers and
members of the militant movement during the first
few years. It was an unwritten rule that there must be
no concerts, no theatres, no smoking; work and sleep
to prepare us for more work was the unwritten order
of the day . . . I always admired the careful and
methodical way in which the money was spent. That
is why we did so much more with our money than
party politicians. Mere hard work would tell, no
money was spent on advertising. If a chair would be
suitable as a platform why pay a few shillings for a
trolley? If the weather was fine why hire a hall? If the
pavements were dry, why not chalk advertisements of
the meeting instead of paying printers bills? If a
tram would take us, why hire a taxi? This went on for
years . . .

Annie Kenney, **Memories of a Militant**, *1924*

The two separate wings of the women's
suffrage movement – the WSPU and NUWSS
– worked hard to put their message across to
politicians and the general public alike.
Despite the differences in policy and style, the
two organisations worked well together, at
least in the early years. Mrs Fawcett, President
of the NUWSS, praised the bold tactics of the
WSPU: 'In my opinion, far from having
injured the movement they have done more
during the last twelve months to bring it
within the region of practical politics than we
have been able to accomplish in the same
number of years'. For the first time in nearly
half a century the issue of votes for women was
getting serious attention and coverage from the
Press, thanks largely to the flamboyant style of
the WSPU.

*The Woman's Press. The merchandising of the WSPU's
message had been so successful that in 1910 The Woman's
Press opened a new shop at 156 Charing Cross Road,
London.*

'Deeds not Words' was the WSPU's new
slogan, and a new style for the 20th century
struggle. The well-established women's suffrage
movement was injected with new life by
women who were no longer prepared to wait
passively for politicians to act. The
government was about to be attacked on
many different fronts by respectable women in
a way which would have been unthinkable
even just a few years before.

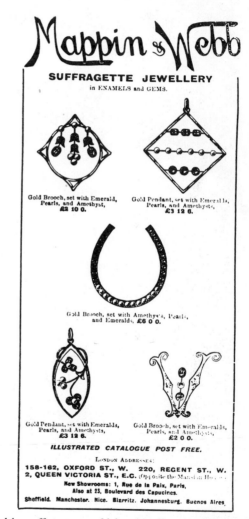

*Wealthy suffragettes could buy jewellery specially made by
Mappin and Webb in the three colours of the movement –
purple, white and green.*

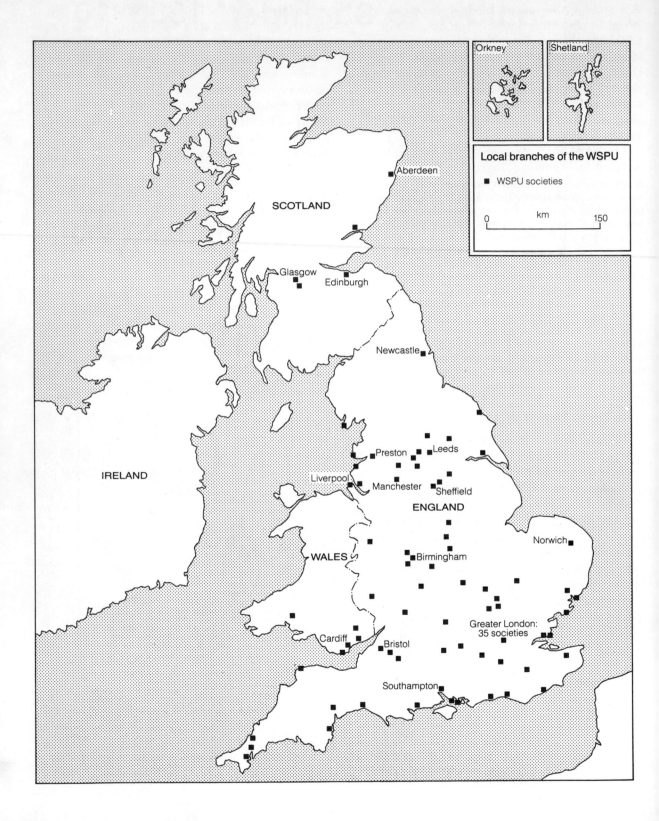

5 'Shoulder to Shoulder' 1906–10

As you read in the last two chapters, both the suffragists and the suffragettes wanted votes for women. Whereas the suffragists campaigned peacefully, the suffragettes were prepared to break the law. Most political campaigns are not straightforward affairs in which the goal is neatly achieved at the end, and the struggle for votes for women was no exception. It was a story of many victories and just as many setbacks, yet it was a campaign to which both groups of women were strongly committed.

In May 1906 the new Liberal Prime Minister, Sir Henry Campbell-Bannerman finally agreed to see a *deputation* which included a number of suffragists, suffragettes and politicians. At the meeting he blamed his own senior ministers in the Cabinet for the lack of progress, and assured the deputation he was for women's suffrage, whereas his colleagues were divided on the issue. He simply told them to 'carry on pestering'.

Tactics of the NUWSS

The NUWSS were disappointed with the Prime Minister. Many members were keen Liberals, and had expected a firm commitment. But they were not put off and carried on lobbying for support. During July a special campaign was run to put gentle pressure on MPs to try and persuade them to change their minds. Many meetings were held throughout Britain: petitions were collected, and literature was given away free of charge.

In October the NUWSS announced they would put up their own independent male

An office at the WSPU headquarters in London. This office was run by Jessie Kenney, sister of Annie Kenney. The map in the background gives an idea of how nationwide the movement was.

candidates to run against Liberal politicians who were opposed to votes for women. This new and much more aggressive policy was a step forward for the suffragists. For the first time the NUWSS was going out to meet the voters directly to put their message across.

Arrest and imprisonment: tactics of the WSPU

Parliament opened on 23 October 1906. A group of suffragettes arrived at the House of Commons determined to get a promise that women's suffrage would soon be considered. When their request was turned down, several women climbed on to seats in the lobby of the House to make protest speeches, and others linked arms to protect them. The police were called in, and ten women were arrested. They were charged with using threatening and abusive words, and behaviour with intent to provoke a breach of the peace. The women chose to go to prison for two months rather than pay fines. This incident gave the WSPU valuable publicity and new recruits joined the movement.

From 1907 the WSPU began to oppose MPs at by-elections. Their performance as canvassers won them a certain amount of respect:

The women canvass in the rain and engage in competition for open-air audiences. Women draw up lists of speakers and look after the arrangements for vehicles. They carry sandwich-boards, they distribute leaflets and they roar through megaphones and look up all the vacant dates of all the meeting rooms they can find. It may not be 'womanly' but it is done and no Parliamentary candidate can afford to ignore the fact.

Nottingham Guardian, *12 December 1907*

During this campaign, which lasted until the outbreak of the First World War in 1914, the WSPU canvassed at many by-elections. Liberal MPs were defeated, and votes were lost, much to the suffragettes' delight. It is hard to say how many votes, if any, they took away from the Liberals, as voters were influenced by issues other than votes for women. Whatever the result, the WSPU claimed it as their victory.

The Mud March

The NUWSS organised its first London procession for 9 February 1907. It was to show politicians and the general public the demand for women's suffrage. Because of bad weather the demonstration became known as the 'Mud March'. Over 3,000 women marched from Hyde Park to Exeter Hall, in the Strand, accompanied by bands playing music. The banners they carried represented over 40 different womens' organisations. The founder of the Labour Party, Keir Hardie, and well-known writers like H. G. Wells made speeches in support of votes for women. At the time there was a sense of shock at the sight of women marching in this kind of public demonstration.

During 1907 the organisation went from strength to strength. The numbers of staff on the payroll grew, and within eighteen months there were ten full-time paid organisers co-ordinating the campaign nationally and locally.

The WSPU splits

Even though all the members of the WSPU were fighting for the same end, it was inevitable that the different opinions of some individuals would cause conflict. The fight for the vote was seen by many as a life and death struggle. Feelings ran high, and tension often came to the surface.

By the autumn of 1907 there were changes in the WSPU. Mrs Pankhurst and her daughter Christabel were strongly criticised by three senior members of the organisation for their style of leadership. Some of their critics founded a new party, the *Women's Freedom League (WFL)*.

The WFL developed quickly. By 1914 their newspaper, *The Vote*, was well established and there was a membership of about 4,000, in 60 branches in towns throughout Britain. They were a militant organisation which attacked the government, but they also criticised the WSPU's campaign of vandalism against private and commercial property. Over 100 of their members went to prison for various offences committed while protesting against the government's inaction on votes for women. The WFL ran the Women's Tax Resistance League, which was founded in 1909. The policy of refusing to fill in the *Census* forms in 1911 (see page 30) was another campaign of this organisation.

A further example of conflict was when Sylvia Pankhurst was expelled from the WSPU in 1914. Christabel strongly disapproved of her sister's involvement with working-class women, and her organisation, the East London Federation of Suffragettes. Its first headquarters were opened in a disused baker's shop in Bow, and the response from local women was very encouraging.

Sylvia trained speakers, organised poster parades and meetings, and went on several deputations with working-class women. Their headquarters became a centre for social work in the area and their weekly newspaper, *The Woman's Dreadnought*, kept working-class suffragettes informed on the fight for the vote.

Christabel did not approve of this campaign, and when it proved impossible to discipline her sister, Sylvia was told to leave the WSPU. Upset, but undeterred by this,

Women's Freedom League caravan. Horse-drawn caravans like this one toured all over Britain in the summer months throughout the WFL campaign.

Sylvia Pankhurst addressing a crowd outside the WSPU office in Bow, East London, in 1912.

Sylvia and the East London Federation of Suffragettes carried on.

1908: a new Prime Minister – a new enemy

In April 1908 Sir Henry Campbell-Bannerman died, and Herbert Henry Asquith took over as leader of the Liberal government. His views on women's suffrage were well-known: he was a definite 'Anti'. However, in May he agreed to see a deputation of campaigners. He urged them to prove to him that there was a widespread demand for votes for women, and if this was the case then the government would consider a bill in Parliament. So both the suffragists and suffragettes went ahead and organised two huge demonstrations in London,

and others in major provincial cities.

Over 10,000 women took part in the NUWSS procession in London on 14 June 1908. They walked from the Embankment to the Albert Hall where they heard many speeches on the urgent need for women's suffrage. Banners were carried by women from all over Britain. Local suffrage groups worked hard to ensure that as many women as possible went to London. Poorer women had their train fares paid by donations from wealthier NUWSS members. Special trains were chartered, and refreshments were provided for the women before they made their return journey home.

A week later the WSPU staged 'Women's Sunday' in Hyde Park. On 21 June crowds of more than half a million flocked to the

Women's Sunday: one of the seven huge WSPU processions which converged on Hyde Park, London, on 21 June 1908. This one marched past the Houses of Parliament.

The Purple, White & Green.

Oh ! Women dear, and did ye hear the news that's going round,
They think that prison bars will daunt those born on English ground ;
They think they'll pile on penalties far harder than we've seen,
And gag the shouts of those who wear the purple, white and green.
But when we meet you women and you take us by the hand,
And you ask " How are you doing ? " we answer, " doing grand ! "
For it is the grandest movement the world has ever seen,
And we're gath'ring in our thousands, wearing purple, white and green.

For it is the grandest movement the world has ever seen,
And we'll win the Vote for Women, wearing purple, white and green.

For forty years we talked and prayed, as gentle women do,
And oft the Cause has been betrayed by men we counted true ;
But now the woman-worker roused, shouts with insistent note
For what she wants without delay—*and means to have*—the Vote !
So until the House of Commons heeds our knocking at the door,
And grants the freedom women claim, as men have claimed before ;
Until the British woman votes like man for what she pays,
Until *that* day—so help us God !—our protests we will raise.

For it is the grandest movement the world has ever seen,
And we'll win the Vote for Women, wearing purple, white and green.

L. E. MORGAN-BROWNE.

The Purple, White and Green: *one of the many suffrage songs which were sung to popular tunes of the day.*

demonstration. Again, specially chartered trains brought women from all over Britain. Sunday was chosen so that as many working women as possible could attend. Over 700 banners in purple, white and green were carried in seven huge processions to Hyde Park. The wealthier women demonstrators took the wearing of the colours so seriously that department stores in London sold out of white dresses and purple, white and green accessories well before the day. *The Times* reported:

We can but offer a tribute of admiration to the wonderful skill in organisation displayed by those responsible for this remarkable demonstration, and at the same time to the management by the police of this enormous crowd. Certainly, Mr Asquith's advice is bearing fruit. It would be idle to deny, after the object lessons of June 13 and yesterday, that a great many women are for the time being, eagerly desirous of the franchise.

The Times, *22 June 1908*

The first window-smashers

On 30 June 1908 thousands of sympathisers and curious members of the public went to a demonstration organised by the WSPU in Parliament Square, London. Five thousand police were called in to deal with the crowds, and violence broke out. Enraged by the violence in the Square, two teachers, both WSPU members, Mary Leigh and Edith New, took a cab into Downing Street and flung small stones through the windows of the Prime Minister's house.

Twenty-seven women were sent to prison that day, and the first window-smashers served two months in Holloway Prison. When they were released they were treated like heroines by the suffragettes, and a huge breakfast reception was held in their honour.

The summer processions were a great success. The demand for women's suffrage was brought to the attention of the general public. However, Asquith's attitude gave the women grave cause for concern. An adult Suffrage Bill, which would have given more votes to men, was introduced that year and debated (and later defeated) in the House of Commons. Yet there had been no agitation for male suffrage. The NUWSS and WSPU felt annoyed that such a reform could be considered ahead of their demand.

By the autumn of 1908 more frustration was creeping into the suffragette campaign. The suffragettes were angry at Asquith's stalling tactics. They planned a 'rush' on the House of Commons on 13 October. Sixty thousand people gathered in Parliament Square to see a group of suffragettes try to 'rush', or enter, the House of Commons. There were violent clashes with the police, and 24 women and 13 men were arrested. At the end of the day 10 people needed hospital treatment. The *Daily Express* commented:

The time for dealing gently with idle, mischievous women who call themselves 'militant suffragists' has gone by . . . The grave business of the State was held up. Hundreds of policemen were given difficult and unnecessary work. Such things cannot be tolerated . . . Now the country will demand that these women, who incite to disorder and riot, shall be punished with the utmost severity.

Daily Express, *14 October 1908*

Mary Leigh and Edith New. The first window-smashers were greeted as heroines when they were released from Holloway Gaol. They are holding up bread taken from the prison. A huge party was held in their honour.

In the widely-reported trial that followed, Mrs Pankhurst and Flora Drummond were sentenced to three months in prison and Christabel Pankhurst received ten weeks for inciting the public to 'rush' the House of Commons.

Pestering the politicians

Another tactic used by the suffragettes from 1908 onwards was to confront or 'pester' senior Liberal politicians wherever and whenever possible. Very soon women were banned from political meetings unless they had been vetted first.

By the spring of 1909 the WSPU had good reason to feel pleased with its progress. Although the vote for women was no nearer, they were firmly established as a political organisation. With 75 office staff on the payroll, hundreds of unpaid volunteers, and

branches opening up all over the country, the movement was well-off and well run. Their official newspaper, *Votes for Women*, had a weekly circulation of 20,000 and a readership of at least four times that figure.

But at this point many women within the NUWSS felt very pessimistic about the future. MPs who had supported women's suffrage seemed to prefer to work for adult male suffrage instead. Asquith was even more hostile to their demands than ever.

However, the propaganda work of the NUWSS rolled on. As a political organisation it was doing extremely well. In the last two years the number of societies had quadrupled, and the paid up membership had increased from just under 6,000 to well over 13,000. But since the autumn the NUWSS had cooled in its attitude to the WSPU. They were afraid the WSPU's militant activity would lose the movement valuable support in the House of

Commons. Unfortunately their fears proved to be well founded.

During the summer of 1909 the WSPU stepped up its pressure on the government. On 29 June a suffragette deputation tried to see Asquith, but he refused to meet them. While they were being forced back by the police, a small group of women armed with stones smashed government office windows. One hundred and eight women were arrested that day, and fourteen window-smashers were sent to Holloway Prison for a month. Once in prison they were involved in a bitter fight to claim status as political prisoners.

Since the start of the militant campaign there had been a dispute with the authorities over the kind of treatment that suffragette prisoners should be given. The WSPU said its members were involved in a political battle, and if arrested and imprisoned, should be given the status of political prisoners. Some suffragettes were given this treatment, but the government refused to allow special privileges to the vast majority of WSPU prisoners. Once in gaol they were usually treated just like other criminals. In protest at their treatment the first window-smashers went on hunger strike, refusing all food until they were given political status.

The hunger strikes

The prisons now became a new battleground in the fight for votes for women. The authorities did not want any starving women on their hands, and at first released those women who used this tactic. Just a few months later, however, force-feeding was introduced:

Then he [the doctor] put down my throat a tube which seemed to me much too wide, and was something like 4 feet in length. The irritation of the tube was excessive. I choked the moment it touched my throat. Then the food was poured in quickly, it made me sick a few seconds after it was down and the action of the sickness made my body and legs double up, but the wardresses instantly pressed back my head and the doctor leant on my knees.

Lady Constance Lytton, **Prisons and Prisoners**, *1914*

Some women tried to stop the authorities force-feeding them and barricaded themselves into their cells, and on one occasion hosepipes were used to end the protest. Another woman set fire to her cell and was unconscious when rescued. The leadership recognised their courage and awarded medals to those suffragettes who were force-fed.

The Prime Minister and senior politicians were by now openly hostile to the women's demands. The prospect of votes for women seemed remote at the end of 1909. In the early years the NUWSS had not criticised the militants. Mrs Fawcett preferred, 'to keep our artillery for our opponents and not turn it on one another'. Now the NUWSS felt that the militancy of the WSPU was harming the cause. Some old friends of women's suffrage in the House of Commons had been lost. 'Unwomanly' actions like heckling and pestering politicians, hurling missiles at the police and rowdy demonstrations outside halls from which they were banned, had alienated the more cautious sympathisers.

A Highlands welcome in London for Mary Phillips, the Scottish suffragette released from Holloway Goal on 18 September 1908. She had been arrested on 30 June while on a deputation to the House of Commons. Mary Phillips is standing to the left of 'General' Flora Drummond (centre).

VOTES FOR WOMEN

EDITED BY FREDERICK AND EMMELINE PETHICK LAWRENCE.

VOL. III. (New Series), No. 99.   **FRIDAY, JANUARY 28, 1910.**   Price 1d. Weekly. (Post Free. 1½d.)

THE GOVERNMENT'S METHODS OF BARBARISM.

FORCIBLE FEEDING IN PRISON.

In some cases, instead of nasal feeding as in the picture, the still more dangerous practice of feeding through the mouth, by a tube, down the throat, is adopted. This was done in the case of Jane War on.

(This Cartoon is being made into a Poster, which can be obtained separately. Particulars will be found on page 274.)

Front cover of Votes for Women, *28 January 1910.*

6 At last! A bill to work for

The Conciliation Bill, 1910

In 1910 the joint action of the WSPU and the NUWSS eventually persuaded the government to set up a Conciliation Committee to draw up a bill to give votes to women. Hopes were high and Mrs Pankhurst called a halt to all WSPU militant activities.

The Conciliation Committee was made up of a wide cross-section of politicians in the House of Commons. Their job was to draft a bill which would be acceptable to all parties. The NUWSS worked very closely with the Committee. A general election was due at the end of January 1910, and Mrs Fawcett and her colleagues felt that the Liberals would be more willing to listen to the women's demands with an election in mind. In the run up to the election over 300 MPs pledged their support for women's suffrage, and a petition of more than 250,000 signatures was collected and presented to the House of Commons in March. The WSPU 'truce' enabled the Bill to be drafted and debated in a peaceful atmosphere.

In June Mrs Fawcett led a deputation to see Asquith, the Prime Minister. He was very evasive about the new Conciliation Bill. Privately Mrs Fawcett and her colleagues were pessimistic about its chances. It would have to be read twice and passed in the House of Commons as soon as possible, if there was any chance of its becoming law in the near future. The women were worried that Asquith and his supporters would use any chance they could to ruin its chances of success.

The Bill was due for its second reading in July, and the NUWSS worked hard to win further support for it. They were always afraid the WSPU would start up its militant campaign and spoil the Bill's chances of becoming law. Throughout this campaign the NUWSS became very skilful at walking the tightrope between the hostility of Liberal politicians towards women's suffrage, and the hostility of the suffragettes towards those MPs who were Antis. Later, Mrs Fawcett wrote:

Like all moderate parties we were kicked on both sides, and while we had to endure the stones and offal which were frequently hurled at us on their account we were constantly told by 'wobbly' politicians that they could no longer support us unless we somehow stopped the militants.

The Conciliation Bill was read for a second time on 11 and 12 July 1910. In all, 39 speeches were made for and against it. The Antis worked hard against the Bill, using the same arguments of the past 40 years. The Liberal MPs Winston Churchill and Lloyd George spoke sharply against the Bill too. Yet despite opposition from such important politicians, the Bill passed its second reading with a large majority of 100 votes. However, the suffragettes and suffragists were bitterly disappointed when Asquith said that no more time would be given for further discussion of the Bill. He suspended Parliament until November and so the future of the Bill was extremely uncertain. Both sides of the suffrage movement canvassed with a new intensity. Disgusted with the Liberal government, the WSPU called off its truce, and on Friday 18 November, they protested outside the House of Commons.

BLACK FRIDAY
DISORDERLY SCENES AND ARRESTS AT WESTMINSTER

Over 400 suffragettes took part in the demonstration on 18 November 1910 and it quickly turned into a riot. The government had expected trouble and drafted in extra police. They were not experienced at handling women demonstrators, and over 300 women became involved in a bloody fight. The day became known as 'Black Friday'. More than

VOTES FOR WOMEN

The Women's Social and Political Union,
HEAD OFFICE: 4, CLEMENTS INN, STRAND, W.C.
Telegraphic Address: "Wospolu, London."   Telephone No. 2724 Holborn (three lines).

IRISHWOMEN!
Come and join your Countrywomen in the
MONSTER DEMONSTRATION
FROM
WESTMINSTER EMBANKMENT
TO
HYDE PARK
IN SUPPORT OF THE
Votes for Women Bill
SATURDAY, JULY 23rd, at 5.30.

Form up on the Embankment at Cleopatra's Needle at 5 p.m.
Start at 4 p.m.

WSPU handbill, 1910. Irish women from all over Britain were invited to join in the monster demonstration in Hyde Park, London.

150 women were victims of physical and sexual assaults. The Conciliation Committee prepared a report for the government. The following account is typical:

I saw an Inspector run from the cordon over to me. He furiously struck me with his fist and felled me to the ground. I got up, and he said, 'You would strike me', and felled me again. Blood was flowing from the first blow I received . . . while I was lying on the ground a mounted man came so near to me that the hoof of his horse crushed and cut the little handbag that was still hanging from my arm.

Report of the Treatment of Women's Deputation, *Conciliation Committee, 1911*

Feeling was running high, and further riots took place in Downing Street and Parliament Square during the following week. The Home Secretary, Winston Churchill, anxious to avoid the publicity that court cases would bring, dropped most of the charges against the 120 women who were arrested, but rejected all calls for a public inquiry into police brutality.

Renewed truce

Eventually the WSPU called a truce which lasted almost a year. All the women's suffrage campaigners pinned their hopes on the Conciliation Bill becoming law in 1911. During this time the WSPU softened their anti-Liberal approach, and said that if MPs agreed to support the Bill then they would not canvass against them at by-elections. Both the NUWSS and the WSPU were now involved in large peaceful processions, and resisting the Census.

'No Votes, No Census!'

On 2 April 1911, the official Census was taken and hundreds of women's suffrage campaigners refused to take part in the head count of the population. Census forms were not filled in properly or had the slogan 'No Votes, No Census' written across them. Some women stayed away from home on the night Census officials called. All-night parties were organised and large concerts were held in halls and theatres all over Britain. Although the government threatened legal action against the Census resisters, none was taken.

The NUWSS were very optimistic about the chances of the 1911 Conciliation Bill becoming law. Over 150 town and county councils gave firm support to the Bill which was due to be discussed in May. The NUWSS aimed a special propaganda campaign at Irish Nationalist MPs. They were an important group of politicians at Westminster, but unfortunately would make no firm commitment to the women's suffrage movement. Still, despite the lack of interest from the Irish MPs, the Conciliation Bill passed this reading. Everyone was waiting to see how the government would react. Would they help or hinder the Bill?

They stalled, and said there was no time to get the Bill through that session of Parliament. The WSPU, NUWSS and the Conciliation Committee were furious. Their patience was running out. However, they were all reassured by their friends in the government that the Bill would become law during the next session of Parliament and felt optimistic once again. Mrs Fawcett went as far as to say, 'We are higher up the ladder than we have ever been before'.

The Women's Coronation Procession

The summer of 1911 gave the women's suffrage movement a wonderful opportunity to show itself to the country in the best possible light. King George V was due to be crowned in June, and the world's leaders and Press would be in London in large numbers. 'Votes for Women' was to be presented in a peaceful and patriotic way. On 17 June the WSPU held the Women's Coronation Procession. Many other suffragist organisations took part. The procession stretched for seven miles. Bands played music, and over 1,000 banners carried slogans demanding votes for women. Sixty thousand women took part, and a huge meeting was held in the Albert Hall immediately after the procession. This event won the campaigners a great deal of respect. London's evening newspaper, *The Star*, commented:

It proves that women as well as men can contribute together in the common pursuit of a high ideal. It also proves that women are capable of emulating masculine endurance of physical fatigue. Nothing can prevent the triumph of the cause which behind it has such reserves of courage and conviction.

The Star, *19 June 1911*

A new Reform Bill?

In the autumn of 1911 Lloyd George, now Chancellor of the Exchequer, asked the NUWSS to give up the Conciliation Bill and work instead for a new Reform Bill, which would give more votes to men. It was to include an amendment which would allow some form of women's suffrage. In this way some women would get the vote, but only

Indian suffragettes at the Women's Coronation Procession, 17 June 1911.

really as an afterthought to reform which gave more votes to men. The NUWSS thought very carefully about the offer, and in October agreed to work for the new Bill only if it had a women's suffrage amendment. They were worried, however, about how the WSPU would react when they heard the news.

The news broke on 7 November when Asquith saw a group of campaigners who had been working for more votes for both men and women. He told them that the government would introduce a new Reform Bill in the next parliamentary session. He also promised that the government would not oppose the women's suffrage amendment. As the NUWSS feared, the WSPU were furious at the news. They said Lloyd George's actions were treacherous, and they had no faith in the proposed new Bill. In November the WSPU truce was called off for good. Even the Press were shocked at the government's actions. The *Evening Standard* remarked, 'We are no friends of female suffrage but anything more contemptible than the attitude as seen by the government is difficult to imagine' (8 November 1911).

7 'Deeds not Words' 1912–14

Renewal of suffragist disturbances

Patience and optimism gave way to bitter resentment and anger. The next phase of suffragette violence was about to begin. On 21 November 1911, thousands of pounds worth of damage was caused in London when suffragettes smashed the windows of government and private offices, and West End shops. For the first time commercial properties were attacked, and more than 200 women were arrested on that day. Their prison sentences varied from one week to six months. Yet the NUWSS were still optimistic. They felt that only Lloyd George could help their cause. The suffragists were keeping their options open, and worked alongside Socialists, Liberals and women's political organisations in an attempt to drum up support for the new Reform Bill, and as a second option, the Conciliation Bill.

WHOLESALE WINDOW SMASHING IN LONDON

The women's suffrage campaign suffered a humiliating setback early in 1912. The government postponed the new Reform Bill, deciding that the Conciliation Bill was to be discussed first. Senior NUWSS members were afraid that Asquith was once again stalling. On 1 and 4 March the WSPU organised another window-smashing campaign in London. Thousands of pounds worth of property was damaged. Public opinion was outraged. *The Times* commented on 5 March:

Were it not for the calculated and determined manner in which this work of devastation was carried out one would suppose it to have been wrought by demented and maniacal creatures, and even as it is a survey of the scene rather suggests that the mischief was done by people of unstable mental equilibrium . . .

By this time window-smashing was official WSPU policy. After Black Friday, the old style of deputations was replaced by open law-breaking which would guarantee immediate arrest. At a large meeting Mrs Pankhurst warned everyone of the changed mood of the suffragettes: 'To argue with a revolution they will find very futile indeed'. Her reasons for this new policy: 'Our very definite purpose is to create an intolerable situation for the Government, and if need be, for the public as a whole'.

The end of the Conciliation Bill

The NUWSS continued with its usual style of campaigning. They were, however, worried about the chances of the Conciliation Bill becoming law, in the wake of the window-smashing. A Conservative MP wrote to Mrs Fawcett, 'My attitude is shared by over four score of the former supporters of this measure and the damage done to the movement will be seen'.
M. G. Fawcett, **What I Remember**, *1924*

On 28 March, as expected, the Conciliation Bill was defeated, but only by a narrow margin. The Irish Nationalists voted against it, because they wanted any time available for debate to be used to discuss *Home Rule*. Suffragette violence gave politicians the excuse they needed to vote against a reform they opposed. The Conciliation Committee came to an end.

Labour Party support

During 1912 the Labour Party had come round to the idea of supporting votes for women. After much discussion with the Party, the NUWSS announced its Election Fighting Fund. They planned to start a fund which would finance a campaign to help Labour candidates to be elected to the House of Commons. They set their sights on the next General Election, which was expected in 1915.

The Election Fighting Fund was set up in July, and at the same time the Friends of Women's Suffrage scheme was introduced. Women who wanted to join the movement, but were afraid of committing themselves on paper, or could not afford the annual subscription, could still become members of the NUWSS as 'friends'. The scheme was a great success, particularly among working-class women, and by 1914 over 46,000 'friends' had allied themselves with the NUWSS. More working-class women were employed by the NUWSS as organisers, mainly in the industrial areas in the north of England. However, not all NUWSS members were keen on such close ties with the socialist Labour party. They had to be won round, and those who were not happy with the changes left the women's suffrage movement.

Guerrilla warfare

The authorities decided to take action against the WSPU, in the wake of the recent window-smashing campaign. On 5 March 1912, they raided their headquarters at Clement's Inn. Christabel Pankhurst had been 'tipped off' and escaped to Paris before the raid. The Pethick Lawrences were arrested and charged with conspiracy to commit damage. They were to take the blame for suffragette outrages. Even though she was already in prison, Mrs Pankhurst was charged with the same offence. Annie Kenney became Christabel Pankhurst's deputy. Window-smashing gave the government the perfect excuse not to give votes to women. The Pethick Lawrences and Mrs Pankhurst were sentenced to nine months in prison. They demanded political status and

One of the many houses, belonging to political opponents, which was attacked by suffragette bombers and arsonists in 1913 and 1914.

were eventually given it. However, when other suffragettes demanded the same, it was refused, and a mass hunger strike started in prisons all over the country. Their campaign meant that many suffered the horrors of force-feeding.

During 1913 and 1914 suffragette violence increased. Private houses, churches and public places were bombed. Race courses and golf courses had slogans cut and burned into their turf. Telephone and telegraph wires were cut, and three greenhouses at Kew Gardens were wrecked. Thousands of letters were destroyed when chemicals were poured into post boxes. In February 1913 the newly-built Surrey home of Lloyd George was badly damaged by a bomb planted by Emily Wilding Davison. Railway stations, sports pavilions and empty houses were destroyed with home-made devices. But few suffragette bombers were caught, much to the anger of politicians and public alike.

The Cat and Mouse Act 1913

Suffragette prisoners continued to go on hunger strike and demand political status. There was public outcry at the government's force-feeding. In April 1913 the authorities rushed through the *Prisoner's Temporary Discharge for Ill Health Act*. Because of the way this Act operated the WSPU called it the 'Cat and Mouse Act'. Under the terms of the Act hunger strikers or 'mice' were released on special licence by the authorities or 'Cat' for a specific period of time. However, they could then be re-arrested and returned to prison to complete their sentences whenever the authorities or 'Cat' wished. It was hoped that this would demoralise the suffragettes. But the problems of suffragette 'mice' committing further crimes while out on licence was so acute that force-feeding was re-introduced.

The outrage at the Derby

The most dramatic event of 1913 was the protest of Emily Wilding Davison. She went to the Derby horse race at Epsom in Surrey on 4 June, rushed out on to the racecourse, and grabbed the reins of the King's horse, Anmer.

The *Daily Mirror* described the scene:

Anmer struck her with his chest, and she was knocked over screaming. Blood rushed from her nose and mouth. The king's horse turned a complete somersault, and the jockey, Herbert Jones, was knocked off and seriously injured. An immense crowd at once invaded the course. The woman was picked up and placed in a motor car and taken in an ambulance to Epsom Cottage Hospital.

The Daily Mirror, *5 June 1913*

Emily Wilding Davison died of head injuries on 8 June. Not even her closest friends had any idea of her intentions. The WSPU organised a spectacular funeral procession for Emily Davison. Two thousand suffragettes marched alongside nine bands playing funeral music. Thousands of people turned out to see the procession. Over a thousand wreaths accompanied the body to Northumberland.

The NUWSS and the Women's Pilgrimage

While all this was going on the NUWSS were struggling to keep public opinion on their side. They found it hard to convince everyone that they were not the same as the WSPU. With the background of suffragette violence, the Reform Bill was suddenly withdrawn, in early 1913. The excuse given was the 'problem' of the women's suffrage amendments. Instead of the Bill they had been promised, the campaigners were 'fobbed off' with the promise of a *Private Member's Bill* in the next session of Parliament.

The NUWSS organised the Women's Pilgrimage to try to gain more support for the vote. In June and July 1913 thousands of women took part in a peaceful march to London from all over Britain. The 'pilgrims' set off in the middle of June, and spent six weeks on the road, holding meetings on the way and raising money for their funds. Eight thousand pounds, worth over a quarter of a million pounds today, was raised on the pilgrimage. A few women walked the entire route, but most walked only part of the way.

The marchers sang songs and wore the NUWSS colours, red, white and green. Their weekly newspaper, *The Common Cause*, told members taking part:

Women at the end of their Pilgrimage, 1913. There was a blaze of colour – the NUWSS colours of red, white and green – as women and men entered Hyde Park, London. The 'pilgrims' had spent six weeks on the road, raising funds for the cause.

Every pilgrim must wear the hat badge which is the hallmark of our constitutional pilgrimage . . . We should like to ask every member of the NUWSS to make a point of never appearing in public without the colours. We want the public during the coming weeks to see and read of the red, white and green wherever they turn.

The Common Cause, *July 1913*

The Times reported the arrival of the pilgrims in London on 26 July:

On Saturday the pilgrimage of the law abiding advocates of votes for women ended in a great gathering in Hyde Park attended by some 50,000 persons. The proceedings were quite orderly and devoid of any untoward incident . . . the proceedings, indeed, were as much a demonstration against militancy as one in favour of women's suffrage. Many bitter things were said of the militant women.

The Times, *26 July 1913*

'Wild Women'

As long as the government continued to force-feed WSPU prisoners, suffragette violence was kept at fever pitch. Doctors who did not denounce force-feeding had their windows smashed, and a prison doctor who worked at Holloway Prison was attacked on his way to work by suffragettes wielding a rhino whip. As the violence increased attitudes hardened on both sides.

SLASHER MARY
SUFFRAGETTE SLASHES £45,000 VENUS

This *Daily Mirror* headline appeared on 1 March 1914. The newspaper told of Mary

Richardson's attack on the Rokeby Venus painting by Velasquez at the National Gallery: 'A suffragette armed with a meat cleaver yesterday perpetrated one of the most senseless and savage outrages in the wild women's campaign'. 'Slasher Mary', as the newspapers called her, had been outraged at the number of times Mrs Pankhurst had been arrested and released under the terms of the Cat and Mouse Act. She received eighteen months in prison, with a recommendation of hard labour.

Incidents like this closed many of the country's art galleries and museums to the public completely, or sometimes to women only. At places of historical interest the rule of 'No muffs, wrist bags or sticks' was widespread. Later, in May, the Royal Academy and the Tate Gallery in London closed to the public. The British Museum was more flexible:

The British Museum is open to men, and also to women if accompanied by men who are willing to vouch for their good behaviour and take full responsibility. Unaccompanied women are only allowed in on presentation of a letter of introduction from a responsible person vouching for the bearer's good behaviour and accepting responsibility for her acts.

Any solutions?

Anger at continued suffragette violence drove some members of the public to take revenge. WSPU shops in Bristol, Birmingham and Newcastle were smashed up and there were some terrifying incidents. The *News of the World* reported:

Three young men meeting in a suburb, a woman who was carrying a can of tar and suffragist literature, approached and asked her if she was a suffragist. This being admitted, the men, it is reported, tore off nearly all her clothing, saturated it with tar and set fire to it, then they decamped leaving the suffragist to wander about until she was able to obtain some clothing . . .

News of the World, *11 April 1913*

Reginald McKenna, the Home Secretary, angry with the hunger-striking prisoners, suggested the following options to the House of Commons:

The first is to let them die. That is, I should say, at the present moment the most popular, judging by the

'Slasher Mary' leaving court in March 1914.

number of letters I have received. The second is to deport them, the third is to treat them as lunatics, and the fourth is to give them the franchise . . . I think we should not adopt any of them.

During 1914 the general public became even more outraged at the actions of the WSPU. *The Times* reported:

On Saturday night two women distributing suffragist literature at Lyon's Corner House [a restaurant], in Coventry St, Piccadilly, were pelted with cutlery, sugar, bread and cake. The suffragettes were eventually placed in the lift. In the hall however hundreds of diners were reinforced by people from outside awaiting them. For about a quarter of an hour the women were imprisoned in the lift which was suspended between the ground and first floors, missiles being thrown at them through the cage.

The Times, *24 April 1914*

And yet, in spite of their massive unpopularity, they were still able to hold a fund-raising meeting in London in June, raising what would now be the equivalent of just under a quarter of a million pounds. While suffragette violence was being stepped up, the NUWSS continued to do their bit to win support for a measure of women's suffrage.

Suddenly in the summer of 1914 the women's suffrage campaign stopped. Britain was at war.

8 The First World War and the vote

The women's suffrage campaign stopped more or less completely in August 1914. The First World War, or the Great War as it came to be known, created an emergency which scaled down dramatically the fifty-year struggle which had been waged by the suffragists and the suffragettes. On 10 August the government released WSPU prisoners on the understanding that violence would cease. 'When fighting began', wrote Mrs Fawcett's biographer, 'and when the Germans advanced into Belgium, Mrs Fawcett was one of those who realised that English intervention was inevitable, and with a desperately heavy heart she turned to the consideration of what she and her societies ought to do' (*Ray Strachey, Millicent Garrett Fawcett, 1931*).

The women's response to the war

Within the women's suffrage movement response to the outbreak of war varied enormously. On 4 August Mrs Fawcett sent this message to her followers, 'Women, your country needs you. *Let us show ourselves worthy of citizenship, whether our claim to it be recognised or not*'.

Many members of the NUWSS became involved in war relief work:

The forms of work varied from place to place. Maternity centres, workrooms for unemployed women, hospitality for Belgians, local relief committees, or Red Cross Centres were arranged . . . As time went on the needs changed somewhat. The unemployment problem very soon ceased, and instead there came the great shortage of workers due to the enlistment of so many men. Then it fell to the lot of the societies to supply women recruits for all kinds of work hitherto done only by men.

Ray Strachey, **Millicent Garrett Fawcett**, *1931*

Their Women's Service Bureau, which was opened early in August 1914, was the means of drafting thousands upon thousands of women into new work of the most varied kinds.

However, not all members of the NUWSS were happy with Mrs Fawcett's emphasis on war work. A split soon appeared. Some women were out and out *pacifists*, who opposed all forms of fighting and war work. Others, while admitting the necessity of continuing to fight, tried to encourage early peace.

Mrs Pankhurst, her daughter Christabel, and their followers in the WSPU stopped campaigning for the vote and threw themselves wholeheartedly into anti-German propaganda, and recruiting women war workers for the Home Front. As far as they were concerned Germany had to be defeated at all costs. Out of unswerving patriotism they placed their support, propaganda and recruiting skills at the disposal of the government. Some very patriotic suffragettes were even known to hand out white feathers, the symbol of cowardice, to young men who were not in military uniform! Christabel Pankhurst, who had recently returned from exile in Paris, tells us:

War was the only course for our country to take . . . As suffragettes we could not be pacifists at any price . . . Mother and I declared support of our country. We declared an armistice with the Government and suspended militancy for the duration of the war. We offered our service to the country and called upon all our members to do likewise.

Christabel Pankhurst, **Unshackled**, *1959*

In 1917 the WSPU changed its name to that of The Women's Party, and their newspaper was retitled *Britannia*. Their leaflets give us some idea of suffragette war work: campaigning for the employment of women in munitions factories; and condemning pacifism and workers who went on strike.

Sylvia Pankhurst and many other suffragettes, on the other hand, disagreed with the majority of WSPU members who supported her mother and sister. Throughout the war she continued to campaign for votes for women, and spoke on pacifism and socialism. The organisation she founded in 1914, the East London Federation of Suffragettes, renamed The Worker's Suffrage

Federation in 1915, provided practical help for the poorest people in London's East End who were badly affected by the war. Mother and Infant Welfare clinics and Cost Price restaurants were opened, and small factories employing women who had lost their jobs because of the war were opened and funded by Sylvia's organisation. Her mother and sister were furious at her attacks on war-time *jingoism*, and her left-wing beliefs.

Charlotte Despard, President of the Women's Freedom League, was appalled at the outbreak of the First World War. She bitterly criticised Britain's involvement and urged the members of her organisation to demonstrate against 'this cruel war'. The WFL was one of the few suffragist societies which continued to campaign for votes for women from 1914 to 1918. Given the fact that huge numbers of women were involved on the Home Front, she fought for equal pay for their war work, and founded the Women's Suffrage National Aid Corps to help women and children in distress. Like other suffragist groups, the WFL opened cheap cafes, milk depots, and clinics for mothers and children

Women signing on for war work. Thousands of women signed on to work in munitions factories during the First World War.

who were most in need. Charlotte Despard's strong pacifist and left-wing beliefs determined WFL policy throughout the war. The women's struggle was not to be sacrificed for the war.

Very many members of the women's suffrage movement were confused at the sharp split in the attitudes of their leaders. Some disliked the jingoism of the newspapers, and as pacifists did not support the war-mongering of Emmeline and Christabel Pankhurst. Others did not like the extent to which Mrs Fawcett was urging women to involve themselves in war work for the Home Front. Nevertheless, thousands of women volunteered for a wide variety of war work.

Women's war work

By the end of the war about one million more women were at work than had been in the summer of 1914. Most of them were taking jobs previously done by men who were in the armed forces. The large number of working-class women was nothing new; such women had always gone out to work. But for the first time middle-class women earning a living became highly visible. Women from all social classes helped the war effort by doing jobs such as heaving coal, portering, labouring in the fields and working in munitions factories. An enormous range of semi-skilled and labouring jobs was taken up by women, who previously would not have been allowed or considered themselves able to do such work. By the end of the war, women had demonstrated that they were *not* weak, frail, unintelligent creatures. They had helped to win the war, and at the same time, overturned society's views about men's and women's roles.

The vote at last

The first positive moves towards votes for women were made during the First World War. Thousands of men who had volunteered to fight for their country had accidentally lost the right to vote. This was potentially embarrassing to the government, so plans were made to give them back their vote: and, to reward women for their war work, to give a limited measure of women's suffrage. An All Party Conference made several recommendations which were eventually included in the *Representation of the People Act*. This, the first act to give votes to women in Britain, became law in February 1918.

Under this Act women over the age of 30 got the vote if they were householders, the wives of householders, occupiers of property with an annual rent of £5, and graduates of British universities, or women who were qualified but not graduates. And so, about eight and a half million women were able to vote in the 1918 election. At long last some women had the vote. Also, very importantly, women became eligible to stand as MPs. Several suffrage campaigners stood for Parliament in the first general election after the war in 1918. None were successful.

The women's suffrage campaigners had hoped that women over the age of 21, like men, would be given the vote. The government was wary of doing this, for two reasons. Firstly, if all women of 21 and over had been given the vote, then they would have outnumbered male voters in an election. Secondly, they felt that women under 30 were too 'flighty' and not responsible enough to choose an MP.

How far women's war work affected the issue of women being granted the vote has been debated a great deal. It was difficult for the government to refuse to give the vote to women who had contributed to the war effort. Many of the arguments of the Antis seemed rather silly in the aftermath of the war. However, it was not just the war which had changed politicians' minds on women's suffrage. The *Coalition Government* which came into office in May 1915 and remained until the end of the war, contained several politicians who were *pro* women's suffrage. Asquith resigned in 1917 and was replaced by Lloyd George, who by this time was more sympathetic to the women's claim. Political opinion came round to support a limited form of women's suffrage. The fact that women had played an important role in the war effort made it easier for politicians to support a bill.

More campaigning ahead

Now that some women had won the vote the leading campaigners went off in different directions. Some gave up their work in politics, while others became involved in other struggles. Annie Kenney and Christabel Pankhurst became extremely religious, and Mrs Pankhurst largely gave up politics. Charlotte Despard and Sylvia Pankhurst became more involved in left-wing causes and Mrs Pethick Lawrence fought for the second instalment of votes for women. She was joined by many members of the NUWSS, which in 1919 changed its name to the National Union of Societies for Equal Citizenship (NUSEC). Some of their other campaigns included equal pay, fairer divorce laws, family allowances and opening up the professions to women.

Women were helped enormously by the *Sex Disqualification Removal Act*, 1919, which made it illegal to exclude them from jobs because of their sex. This meant that they could now become MPs, solicitors, barristers and magistrates. They could also do jury service. Most of the professions were soon to be opened to them, although there was fierce opposition from the Civil Service. The Act removed some very important and long-standing obstacles in the way of equality with men.

The 1920s saw important improvements in the position of women in this country. 'Women's questions' were discussed more seriously in Parliament, helped undoubtedly by the eight female MPs there in 1923. The universities were offering more degrees to a growing number of female students. Divorce laws became more favourable to women, and a campaign for equal pay was waged throughout the 1920s, and beyond (The *Equal Pay Act* was not passed until 1970!). Widows, often the poorest women of all, were given pensions for the first time. Other acts followed which tried to deal with the many inequalities of women's lives.

Votes for all women, 1928

In 1924 the Conservative Government said it would consider the question of votes for more women. Many people felt it was absurd to allow men of over 21 to vote, but not women. In time various groups canvassed for support for the second instalment of votes for women. A bill was introduced in March 1928 and by May it had passed all the stages very easily. There was little serious opposition to the Bill, and it was never in danger of being defeated. Mrs Pankhurst died just before it became law in July 1928.

Mrs Fawcett went to hear the debate in the House of Lords. She went home and wrote:

It is almost exactly 61 years ago since I heard John Stuart Mill introduce his suffrage amendment to the Reform Bill on May 20th, 1867. So I have had extraordinary good luck in having seen the struggle from the beginning.

Ray Strachey, **Millicent Garrett Fawcett**, *1931*

The Bill became law on 2 July 1928. All women over the age of 21 could now vote in elections. Equality in voting rights at last! It was a time of great celebrations.

FREE AND INDEPENDENT.

The Three Leaders (*together*). "WANT A PILOT, MADAM?"
New Voter. "NO, THANKS."

The leaders of the three political parties are keen to offer help and guidance to the young female pilot who has recently been given the vote. The three men are, from left to right: Ramsay MacDonald (Labour), Stanley Baldwin (Conservative) and David Lloyd George (Liberal). Cartoon from Punch, *27 June 1928.*

Lady Nancy Astor, the first woman MP. She came from a wealthy American background. Her husband was the Conservative MP for Plymouth. In 1919 she won the by-election and took over his seat in the House of Commons, after he inherited his father's title and became a member of the House of Lords. She was an MP for 25 years and campaigned vigorously for a variety of women's issues.

Conclusion

The women's suffrage campaign made a huge impact on Edwardian society on many different levels. Women proved their strength in fund-raising, propaganda, organisation and publicity stunts. Behind it all lay hard work, and huge commitment to a cause. Their message had spread far and wide. By the outbreak of the First World War supporters could buy the militant newspapers *The Suffragette* in Paris, Vienna and New York. The view of suffragists as cold, sexually-frustrated, 'masculine' women seemed ludicrous when people could point to the Pankhurst family and many other organisers. The diehard prejudices about Amazonian suffragettes looked ridiculous. Christabel Pankhurst enjoyed the irony of the situation:

The Amazons [a race of strong female warriors] were upon them, yet not fierce and fearsome looking persons, but (and that was the worst of it from the Government's point of view) unaggressive and quite amiable looking women.

Christabel Pankhurst, **Unshackled**, *1959*

Suffragette tactics have come in for a lot of discussion. The greatest value of their methods lay in the publicity they achieved, and the funds and recruits they drew in. However, their campaign of arson, window-smashing, bombing and widespread vandalism alienated a great deal of public opinion. Much of the sympathy and outrage at the government's practice of force-feeding, and the enforcement of the Cat and Mouse Act, evaporated when newspaper headlines told of suffragette terrorism. The British public began to feel that by their deliberate law-breaking, the suffragettes brought all punishments upon themselves. The government did not want to be seen to be giving in to extremism.

Damage which ran into huge sums of money ensured that the government would maintain its entrenched 'no compromise' position. Also, the Liberals had other issues to deal with. The Edwardian years presented several major domestic crises for them; a huge struggle with the House of Lords, the question of Home Rule for Ireland and a series of major industrial disputes. Certain members of the government were seriously afraid of widespread unrest, or even revolution. Therefore, put in this context, the women's suffrage movement was perceived as a smaller, though exceedingly irritating problem, which simply had to join a growing list of political concerns.

During the suffrage campaign important challenges were made to traditional prejudices and stereotypes. Society was being shocked into reappraising women, and their wider roles for the future. Often criticism of the suffragettes in particular revolved just as much round their 'unwomanliness', as the political demands they were making. *The Times* voiced an opinion which must have been shared by many people at the time: 'When women unsex themselves they forfeit all rights to greater consideration'.

The sex barrier which was breached in 1918 was completely removed in 1928. The very worst fears of the Antis were seen to be groundless, and a bill for votes for all women was passed with ease. The struggle which had lasted for three-quarters of a century was over.

9 Case studies

Selina Cooper
Radical Suffragist

Selina Cooper (née Coombe) was born in the west of England, into a large and poor working-class family. When she was young the family moved to Lancashire. Her father, who had been a railway *navvy*, died in 1876, and left them in a desperate financial situation. As a child she worked as a *half-timer* in a cotton mill; at 13 she became a full-time cotton worker, and for many years she worked in Nelson, Lancashire. In 1896 she married Robert Cooper, a cotton weaver, a self-educated man who was a Socialist and a firm believer in votes for women. Also, in that year her career as a public speaker began. Selina Cooper soon became one of the top NUWSS speakers in the north of England.

In 1899 Selina Cooper worked hard to collect signatures for the petition of Lancashire textile women workers, and she accompanied this petition to London. In 1903 she formed the *Nelson and Colne Women's Suffrage Committee*, and for the next ten years she travelled all over Britain, organising and speaking at meetings, and canvassing from door to door to get support for votes for women.

Selina Cooper became a full-time paid organiser for the NUWSS in 1907, and also had close ties with the Pankhursts, although she never agreed with their militant policy and tactics. So valuable was she to the NUWSS that they paid a housekeeper to look after her husband and daughter so that she could continue to work for them. In 1913 she met up with friends who had walked from Lancashire to London in the Women's Pilgrimage. She was one of the speakers at the meeting in Hyde Park on the day the pilgrims arrived, sharing a platform with Mrs Fawcett. She was a very popular woman, who was well-respected among the senior members of the NUWSS.

During the First World War Selina Cooper worked full-time for the NUWSS, doing relief

Selina Cooper (1864–1946)

work to help those who had lost their jobs, many of whom were female cotton workers badly affected by the war. It was a time of personal conflict in her life: while she wanted to help local women in a practical way she did not agree with the patriotic attitude of the NUWSS to the war. She was a committed pacifist, and spoke openly on the urgent need for international peace. In the 1920s she became a magistrate, and in the 1930s was a *Poor Law Guardian* in Burnley. During the Second World War she was an outspoken anti-fascist.

Eleanor Rathbone
Suffragist

Eleanor Rathbone was from a wealthy middle-class family. Her father was the local MP for Liverpool. She was a brilliant student at Somerville College, Oxford. Shortly after leaving university she joined the women's suffrage movement in Liverpool, and became the Honorary (unpaid) Secretary of the local suffrage society, and held the same post on the Women's Industrial Council, an organisation

Eleanor Rathbone (1872–1946)

which investigated working women's wages. In 1909 and 1910 she served on Liverpool City Council (the first woman to do so) and was at the same time a senior member of the national *executive committee* of the NUWSS, and a close friend of Mrs Fawcett. She was a very good public speaker and was one of the most prominent suffragists in north-west England. In 1912, unhappy with the close links of the NUWSS with The Labour Party, she resigned, but returned after a short while.

During the war Eleanor Rathbone supported Mrs Fawcett's patriotic leadership of the NUWSS, and it was during this period that she became concerned with the need for widows' pensions and family allowances. She also did a great deal of social work in the slum districts of Liverpool. She became President of the NUWSS (renamed NUSEC) in 1919, and remained so until 1928. In 1929 she became an Independent MP in the House of Commons.

Emmeline Pethick Lawrence
Suffragette

Emmeline Pethick Lawrence was born in Somerset and came from a wealthy middle-class family. She developed a strong social conscience, and worked hard to help improve the lives of working-class women. From 1890

to 1895 she worked as a 'sister of the people' in the West London Mission. In 1895 she and a friend, Mary Neal, started the Esperance Girls' Club and Social Settlement, a co-operative dressmaking business. Unusually for the time, the women workers were paid a minimum wage of fifteen shillings a week, worked an eight hour day, and were given a paid annual holiday.

In 1906 she joined the WSPU and was a brilliant fund-raiser. In six years she raised the equivalent of well over £3 million to finance the suffragette campaign. She went to prison four times for her WSPU activities; including leading a demonstration at the House of Commons in 1906 and for conspiracy to smash windows in London, in 1912. While in prison she went on hunger strike and was force-fed.

After disagreements with the Pankhursts she and her husband were thrown out of the WSPU. The Pethick Lawrences were very unhappy at the widespread vandalism and arson campaign openly encouraged by Mrs Pankhurst and her daughter Christabel. They still continued to edit the newspaper *Votes for Women*, but after the split with the Pankhursts it was no longer the official paper of the WSPU. They continued their work for women's suffrage and founded the Votes for Women Fellowship.

During the First World War, Emmeline

Emmeline Pethick Lawrence (1867–1954)

Pethick Lawrence was a pacifist, and worked hard for the women's international peace movement. She was also involved in the campaign to get the vote for women in those states of America which had not yet won the vote. In 1918, in the first general election after the war, when some women were able to stand as MPs, she stood, unsuccessfully, as a Labour candidate. For the rest of her life she worked for international peace, and reform in women's welfare.

Hannah Mitchell
Suffragette

Hannah Mitchell (née Webster) was born into a poor Derbyshire farming family, and as a young girl worked as a domestic servant and a dressmaker. When she got married in 1895 she was living in Bolton, in the heart of the cotton belt in north-west England. Both she and her husband were interested in socialism and votes for women. She joined the Women's Co-operative Guild, and in 1903 was one of the earliest recruits to the WSPU when it was founded in Manchester. She became a close friend of the Pankhurst family and Annie Kenney, a woman from the same background as herself. Hannah Mitchell joined the WSPU's team of speakers, and travelled all over Lancashire and Yorkshire, drumming up support for votes for women, selling suffragette literature, and canvassing from door to door. She was also active in the Independent Labour Party at this time, and was a Poor Law Guardian in Ashton-under-Lyne. Her own experience of poverty, and her work as a Guardian increased her commitment to socialism. In her autobiography, *The Hard Way Up*, she remarked that she and other working-class suffragettes worked, 'with one hand tied behind us'. They very often had three jobs: work in mills or factories for wages; their suffrage work; and domestic chores at home.

In 1906 Hannah Mitchell spent three days in Strangeways Prison, Manchester, for obstruction and assaulting a policeman. Later that year she went to London for the first time and was a member of the deputation organised by Sylvia Pankhurst to see the Prime Minister, Sir Henry Campbell-Bannerman. In 1906 she

Hannah Mitchell (1871–1956)

became a paid organiser of the WSPU, until a year later when she had a nervous breakdown and left the organisation. When her health recovered she joined the Women's Freedom League and became a paid organiser for them. While the WFL was a militant organisation, it was far more moderate in style and tactics than the WSPU. She always distanced herself from the extremism of the movement, and was very much against the arson and vandalism of the suffragettes.

After the war she worked for the second measure of women's suffrage which was granted in 1928. She sat on Manchester City Council in the 1920s, and for twenty years was a city magistrate.

In *The Hard Way Up*, Hannah Mitchell tells us:

Men are not so single minded as women are; they are too much given to talking about their ideals, rather than working for them. Even as Socialists they seldom translate their faith into works, being still conservative where women are concerned. Most of us who were married found that Votes for Women were of less interest to our husbands than their own dinners. They simply could not understand why we made such a fuss about it.

Women's suffrage in other countries

1869–1918	Twenty States and one Territory of the USA
1881	Isle of Man
1893	New Zealand
1893–1909	States of Australia
1906	Finland
1907	Norway
1915	Iceland
1915	Denmark
1917	USSR
1918	Germany
1918	Poland
1918–1928	Great Britain
1919	Netherlands
1919	Luxembourg
1919	Czechoslovakia
1919–1921	Sweden
1920	Canada
1920	Austria
1920	Belgium
1922	India
1922	Eire
1929	Ceylon
1930	South Africa
1930	Greece
1931	Portugal
1932	Spain
1934	Brazil
1945	France
1945	Hungary
1945	Italy
1945	Japan
1946	Rumania
1946	Venezuela
1947	Argentina
1947	Bulgaria
1947	Malta
1948	Israel
1952	Mexico
1954	Colombia
1955	Peru
1971	Switzerland
****	Women in Lichtenstein still do not have the vote

Further reading

Adam Ruth, *A Woman's Place, 1910–75*, Chatto and Windus, 1975

Adams Carol, *Ordinary Lives*, Virago, 1982

Atkinson Diane, *Suffragettes*, HMSO, 1988

Atkinson Diane, *Votes for Women Document Pack*, Elm Publications, 1986

Cullen Owens Rosemary, *Smashing Times: a History of the Irish Women's Suffrage Movement 1889–1922*, Attic Press, Dublin, 1984

Garrett Fawcett Millicent, *The Women's Victory and After: Personal Reminiscences 1911–18*, Sidgwick and Jackson, 1920

Garrett Fawcett Millicent, *What I Remember*, 1924

Hart Heber, *Women's Suffrage and the National Danger*, 1889

Liddington and Norris, *One Hand Tied Behind Us: the Rise of the Women's Suffrage Movement*, Virago, 1978

Liddington J., *The Life and Times of a Respectable Rebel, Selina Cooper 1864–1946*, Virago, 1984

Mitchell G. (ed.), *The Hard Way Up: the Autobiography of Hannah Mitchell*, Virago, 1968

Nield Chew Doris, *Ada Nield Chew: the Life and Times of a Working Woman*, Virago, 1982

MacKenzie Midge, *Shoulder to Shoulder: a Documentary*, Penguin, 1975

Page Kathy, *The Unborn Dreams of Clara Riley*, Virago, 1987

Pankhurst Christabel, *Unshackled: the Story of How We Won the Vote*, Hutchinson, 1959

Pankhurst Emmeline, *My Own Story*, the autobiography of Emmeline Pankhurst, 1914, reprinted Virago, 1979

Pankhurst Richard, *Sylvia Pankhurst: Artist and Crusader*, Paddington Press, 1979

Pankhurst Sylvia, *The Suffragette*, Gay and Hancock, 1911

Pankhurst Sylvia, *The Suffragette Movement*, 1931, reprinted Virago, 1977

Raeburn Antonia, *The Militant Suffragettes*, Michael Joseph, 1973

Rosen Andrew, *Rise Up Women: the Militant Campaign of the WSPU 1903–14*, Routledge and Kegan Paul, 1974

Strachey Ray, *The Cause: a Short History of the Women's Movement in Great Britain*, 1931, reprinted Virago, 1978

Strachey Ray, *Millicent Garrett Fawcett*, John Murray, 1931

Tremain Rose, *The Fight for Freedom for Women*, Ballantine Books, New York & London, 1973

Wright Sir A. E., *The Unexpurgated Case against Woman Suffrage*, Constable and Co, 1913

More advanced books

Castle B., *Sylvia and Christabel Pankhurst*, Penguin, 1987

Dangerfield G., *The Strange Death of Liberal England*, Paladin, 1966

Fulford R., *Votes for Women*, Faber and Faber, 1958

Garner L., *Stepping Stones to Women's Freedom: Feminist Ideas in the Women's Suffrage Movement 1900–18*, Heinemann, 1984

Harrison B., *Separate Spheres: the Opposition to Women's Suffrage in Britain*, Croom Helm, 1978

Hollis P., *Women in Public: the Women's Movement 1850–1900*, Allen and Unwin, 1975

Kamm J., *Rapiers and Battleaxes*, Allen and Unwin, 1966

Koss S., *Asquith*, Hamish Hamilton, 1976

Mitchell D., *Women on the Warpath: the Story of Women in the First World War*, Jonathan Cape, 1965

Morgan D., *Suffragists and Liberals: the Politics of Women's Suffrage in England*, Basil Blackwell, 1975

Parker Hume L., *The National Union of Women's Suffrage Societies, 1897–1919*, Garland Publishing, New York, 1982

Riemer E. and Rout J., *European Women: a Documentary History 1789–1945*, Harvester, 1980

Rover C., *Women's Suffrage and Party Politics in Britain, 1866–1914*, Routledge and Kegan Paul, 1967

Rubinsten D., *Before the Suffragettes: Women's Emancipation in the 1890s*, Harvester Press, 1986

Vicinus M. (ed.), *Suffer and Be Still: Women in the Victorian Age*, Methuen, 1972

Vicinus M. (ed.), *The Widening Sphere: Changing Roles of Victorian Women*, Methuen, 1972

Wiltsher A., *Most Dangerous Women: Feminist Peace Campaigners of the Great War*, Pandora, 1985

Questions

Look at the front covers of *Votes for Women* (page 28) and *The Suffragette* (page 4). They are both examples of propaganda.
- What do you think the artist's motives were in both pictures?
- In what ways are these pictures similar?
- In what ways are they different?

2 Look through the book and find three other examples of visual propaganda.
- What were the motives behind the use of this propaganda?
- What was/is the value of this propaganda to: the women's suffrage movement; the general public of the time; an historian?

3 Look at the picture of Women's Sunday on page 24.
- What is the building in the background and what was its importance to the suffrage movement?
- Comment on the proportion of women and men in this picture.

4 Do the pictures in this book give a fair representation of the kind of woman who joined the suffrage movement? Give reasons for your answer.

5 Look at the maps on pages 14 and 20.
- Which organisation had more branches?
- Where were the WSPU and NUWSS branches most concentrated?

6 Find out more about the women's suffrage movement in your own area. The library and local history museum will be very helpful in this research. Were there any women like Ada Nield Chew or Emmeline Pethick Lawrence in your locality?

7 Try to find out more by further reading about the relationship between Mrs Pankhurst and her daughters Christabel and Sylvia. Write a short meal-time conversation between these three women in 1913, and try to re-create the points they would have made about how the movement should proceed.

8 Look at Chapter 6. Devise a meeting between Asquith, the NUWSS and the WSPU, to discuss the Conciliation Bill of 1910. What points would each group have put forward?

9 Divide the class into groups and construct a debate concerning the WSPU's window-smashing campaign of March 1912. What would all the arguments have been for and against this kind of protest?

10 'The need for a large number of women to work for the home front in the First World War gave the government the opportunity to give in to the suffragettes without seeming to do so, by basing the argument on how well the "ladies" had done.' Discuss this argument.

11 What difference did it make for women to have the vote? Give as many examples as you can.

12 Find out about the present-day campaign at Greenham Common in Berkshire. What similarities and differences do you notice between the way the police and newspapers have treated these campaigners, and how they treated women campaigning for the vote.

13 Find out more about other single-issue campaigns, such as: Animal rights; Greenpeace; Plaid Cymru; American Civil Rights Movement.
Choose a campaign, collect its literature, and find out about its history, its aims, methods and to what extent it has been successful. Suggest new materials and schemes which they could use.

14 Are the methods which were used by the suffragettes effective in changing government policy? Can you think of any other organisations which have used, or still use, similar tactics?
Do you think governments should give in to such tactics?

15 Find out about men and women's pay today. Do women get equal pay for equal work?

Glossary

anti someone who is against an idea

bill a proposal for reform presented by MPs to Parliament. If it is agreed upon by the House of Commons and the House of Lords then it becomes an act, and then law

by-election an election held in a constituency to choose a new MP when the previous MP has resigned or died

Cabinet the Prime Minister and senior ministers who are responsible for making and carrying out government policy

census the headcount of the population, held in the first year of every decade. The first census of England and Wales was taken in 1801

coalition government government by an alliance or coalition of political parties who govern the country

deputation a small group of people chosen to represent others at a meeting

executive committee a group of people who run an organisation and make decisions

feminist someone who believes in improving women's rights

franchise the right to vote in a parliamentary election

half-timer a child who spent half a day at work in a cotton mill, and the other half at school, until it left at the age of 13

Home Office government department which is responsible for maintaining law and order, immigration control, and other domestic affairs

Home Rule self-government by a separate Parliament to manage internal affairs. Irish nationalists were demanding a separate Parliament for Ireland

jingoism very strong patriotic and militaristic point of view

Metropolitan Police The police force for London

navvy a labourer, originally someone who built the navigation canals

NUWSS National Union of Women's Suffrage Societies, a union of moderate campaigners for votes for women

pacifist someone who is opposed to war and believes all war to be wrong

Poor Law Guardian a representative of the Central Poor Law Board who was elected by ratepayers to deal with helping the poor

Private Member's Bill a bill put forward by an individual MP in favour of an idea

pro in favour of an idea

radical extreme in politics

radical suffragist suffragist campaigners who fought for working-class women's right to vote

suffrage the right to vote in parliamentary elections

suffragist a person who fought for the right to vote in a peaceful way

suffragette a person who fought for the vote in a militant and violent way

WFL Women's Freedom League, a new party founded in 1907 by former members of the WSPU who were critical of the WSPU's violent methods

Women's Co-operative Guild an organisation founded in 1883 as an offshoot of the co-operative movement. By the turn of the century it had over 12,000 working-class members in nearly 300 branches throughout the country, campaigning for better wages, better education and votes for women

WSPU Women's Social and Political Union, a union of militant campaigners for votes for women